Five Practices:
Extravagant Generosity

five Practices
Extravagant Generosity

Robert Schnase

Abingdon Press
Nashville

FIVE PRACTICES:
EXTRAVAGANT GENEROSITY

Copyright © 2008 by Robert Schnase

This book is printed on acid-free paper.

ISBN 978-1-426-70005-7

08 09 10 11 12 13 14 15 16 17—10 9 8 7 6 5 4 3 2 1
MANUFACTURED IN THE UNITED STATES OF AMERICA

CONTENTS

WELCOME

Dear Friends,

Thank you for participating in this conversation and planning. What you are doing is extraordinarily important for leading your congregation. Vibrant, growing, fruitful congregations practice Radical Hospitality, Passionate Worship, Intentional Faith Development, Risk-Taking Mission and Service, and Extravagant Generosity. These are the fundamental activities that are so critical to fulfilling the mission of the church that failure to practice them in an exemplary way leads to congregational decline. These five are interconnected and all are essential. By repeating, improving, and deepening these practices, congregations fulfill their mission of making disciples of Jesus Christ for the transformation of the world. Congregations invite and welcome people, allow God to shape hearts and minds in worship, offer opportunities for people to grow in grace and in the knowledge of God, provide channels for service to relieve suffering, and help people grow in the grace of giving.

You've been invited to focus particularly on the practice of Extravagant Generosity in your congregation and to turn these edgy and provocative words into ideas, initiatives, plans, strategies, and actions. Throughout the next few weeks, you'll ask, "How are we doing at honoring and loving God and neighbor through our giving? And how could we do better?" Perhaps your congregation already does many things well, and some things very well. Even so, let me invite you to strive for excellence and greater fruitfulness and to open yourself to exploring and learning how to do better.

When elementary-age Little League baseball players practice their sport, they practice batting, catching pop-ups, scooping up ground balls. When professional Major

WELCOME

League players practice—adults at the height of their athletic abilities—what do they do? They practice batting, catching pop-ups, scooping up ground balls. Players at all stages and abilities repeat and deepen and improve upon the same basic practices. The same is true for congregations. The greatest difference between stagnant and declining congregations and those that are continually growing is that in fruitful congregations, the pastor and staff are constantly learning, the leaders and volunteers are constantly learning, and even the members and guests are practicing and improving the basic elements of ministry.

For the next few weeks, ask God to open your heart and mind to new learnings and possibilities for your church. Share honestly, listen carefully, think creatively, and plan courageously together with others in your group. Prepare yourself by praying and by reading the sessions and answering the questions. Attend every gathering, listen to others, learn from examples, and boldly offer new ideas. Commit yourself and your church to offering your utmost and highest for the purposes of ministry in Christ's name. Enjoy doing ministry in the Spirit of Christ, and do all things to the glory of God.

Yours in Christ,

Robert Schnase
Author, *Five Practices of Fruitful Congregations*

Radical Hospitality
Passionate Worship
Intentional Faith Development
Risk-Taking Mission and Service
Extravagant Generosity

Five Practices of Fruitful Congregations

Generosity enlarges the soul, realigns priorities, connects people to the body of Christ, and strengthens congregations to fulfill Christ's ministries. **Giving reflects the nature of God.** Growing in the grace of giving is a response Christian disciples offer to God's call to make a difference in the world.

People who give generously to the church do so because they genuinely desire to make a positive difference for the purposes of Christ and because they want to align their lives with higher purposes.

They give because they:
- **love God**
- **love the church**
- **desire to grow in love of neighbor**

Generosity is an aspect of character. The opposite of generosity is selfishness, self-centeredness, greed, self-absorbed. Generosity extends beyond just the use of money, although it most definitely includes that. There are people generous with their time, with their teaching, with their love. Generosity also finds many biblical sources, and is even mentioned as a gift of the Spirit.

Vibrant, fruitful, growing congregations practice Extravagant Generosity. These churches teach, preach, and practice proportional giving with a goal toward tithing.

Churches that model Extravagant Generosity give joyously, generously, and consistently in ways that enrich the souls of members and strengthen the ministries of the church.

As people grow in relationship to Christ, they grow also in the practice of Extravagant Generosity, offering more of themselves for the purposes of Christ and providing the resources that strengthen ministry and that help the church touch the lives of more and more people in the same way their own lives have been transformed by God.

What Does the Bible Say?

Scripture is replete with examples and teachings that focus on possessions, wealth, giving, gifts, generosity, offerings, charity, and sacrifice. Giving is central to Jewish and Christian practice because people perceive God as extravagantly generous, the giver of every good gift, the source of life and love. People give because they serve a giving God.

In the Old Testament, numerous passages underscore the significance of tithing (giving a tenth) and of first fruits (offering the first and best of the harvest, livestock, and income to the purposes of God). In Genesis 14:20, Abram gave a tenth of everything to God; and throughout Leviticus and Deuteronomy, the practice of tithing and first fruits is evident. The Book of Exodus says, "Take from among you an offering to the LORD; let whoever is of a generous heart bring the LORD's offering" (35:5).

Offering money and other possessions to God results from generosity of heart rather than from mere duty and

> "You will be enriched in every way for your great generosity."
> (2 Corinthians 9:11)

obligation. In Proverbs 3:9, people are reminded to "Honor the LORD with your substance and with the first fruits of all your produce." How people use their material resources either honors or dishonors their relationship to God. Generosity aligns one's life with God's purposes.

The prophet Malachi calls upon people to rely genuinely upon God by offering the tithe, implying that when people test God's faithfulness, they find God's presence and promises trustworthy (Malachi 3:8-10). The voices of the prophets ring the warning that people cannot expect material sacrifices alone to please God but that God's reign requires justice, righteousness, and faithfulness (Amos 5:21-24; Micah 6:8).

Jesus' teachings abound with tales of rich and poor, generous and shrewd, givers and takers, charitable and selfish, faithful and fearful. He commends the poor widow putting her two coins in the treasury; giving out of her poverty, she "put in all she had to live on" (Luke 21:1-4). The story upsets expectations

What Does the Bible Say?

Extravagant Generosity

by pointing to proportion rather than amount as the measure of extravagance.

In the story of the farmer who built bigger barns, placing his trust too much in earthly possessions, Jesus asks the spiritually probing question, "And the things you have prepared, whose will they be?" He warns, "Take care! Be on your guard against all kinds of greed; for one's life does not consist in the abundance of possessions" (Luke 12:13-21). **Acquisitiveness does not foster a life rich in God.** And Jesus recounts the parable of the three servants entrusted with varying talents to illustrate God's desire for the faithful to use what has been given to them responsibly and productively. The steward who fearfully buries his talent for safe-keeping is rebuked (Matthew 25:14-30). How people use what they have matters to God.

Jesus chastises the scribes and Pharisees for hypocrisy, tithing while neglecting justice, mercy, and faithfulness. People of God are to practice justice and compassion without neglecting the tithe (Matthew 23:23). The tithe does not fully meet what the gift and demand of God's grace requires of Jesus' followers.

Jesus' unexpected love for Zacchaeus so radically changes the tax collector that he gives his wealth to the poor and to those whom he has wronged. **Giving serves justice and is a fruit of Christ's transforming grace** (Luke 19:1-10).

> "Take from among you an offering to the LORD; let whoever is of a generous heart bring the LORD's offering." (Exodus 35:5)

Even the story of the good Samaritan highlights extraordinary generosity. The Samaritan not only binds up the wounds of the stranger left to die in the road, but he takes the stranger to an inn, pays for the stranger's care, and commits himself to provide for the long-term well-being of the stranger (Luke 10:35). The Samaritan's generosity, like Christ's compassion, knows no bounds.

Beyond all the teachings and parables, the followers of Jesus see in the gracious and costly gift of his sacrifice

What Does the Bible Say?

and death the ultimate self-revelation of God. **The most memorized Scripture of the New Testament expresses the infinite nature of God's gracious love revealed in the gift we have received in Christ: "For God so loved the world that he gave his only Son" (John 3:16).**

In the early church, the followers of Jesus "would sell their possessions and goods and distribute the proceeds to all, as any had need" (Acts 2:45). Paul describes generosity as one of the fruit of the Spirit, alongside love, joy, peace, patience, kindness, faithfulness, gentleness, and self-control (Galatians 5:22).

All Christians practice generosity while some are particularly gifted by the Spirit to give in extraordinary measures. Paul commends the generosity of communities of faith, especially those who remain surprisingly extravagant in their giving during difficult travails. Writing of the churches of Macedonia, he says,

> "For God so loved the world that he gave his only Son." (John 3:16)

"for during a severe ordeal of affliction, their abundant joy and their extreme poverty have overflowed in a wealth of generosity on their part." They "gave according to their means, and even beyond their means, begging us earnestly for the privilege of sharing in this ministry to the saints" (2 Corinthians 8:2-4).

Paul warns those with material means not to set their hopes on the uncertainty of riches but rather on God, who richly provides everything. "They are to do good, to be rich in good works, generous, and ready to share, thus storing up for themselves the treasure of a good foundation for the future, so that they may take hold of the life that really is life" (1 Timothy 6:18-19).

In every Scripture above—Abram with his tithe, the widow giving all she had, Zacchaeus in his transformation, the Samaritan with his compassion, the churches during travails, and God's self-giving in Christ—giving is always *extravagant*, life-changing, and joyous.

Proverbs 3:9:

"Honor the LORD with your substance and with the first fruits of all your produce."

SESSION 1

Planning Sheet

Take time before your first session to think about these questions, and take notes as you read to remind yourself of your responses for the group discussion.

The Joy of Giving

When do you first remember learning about giving to others? Who first modeled generosity for you? _____
_____
_____

What did this first mentor teach you about why you give? What were the benefits of giving for the recipient? For you as the giver? _____
_____
_____

Think of the opportunities you have had to generously give to others. What was the best, most joyful experience you have had in giving? What made it special?
_____
_____
_____

How did it change you? _____
_____

Have you ever received an extravagant gift, something that you needed but didn't expect? What was it like? _____
_____

Planning Sheet

Based on your experience, list three or four things that you know are important in generous giving:

_____ _____

_____ _____

How are these are part of your congregation's giving? _____
_____
_____

Learning to Give

Consider your congregation. Where are people taught about giving and generosity?

Where do children learn? _____
Teens? _____
Adults? _____

How are stories about giving shared in worship, news bulletins, or other places?
_____
_____
_____

Think this week, is there one thing you could do right away to raise awareness of giving opportunities? _____
_____
_____

As you go through the week, meditate on how you have experienced God's extravagant generosity in your life.

What Is Extravagant Generosity?

The practice of generosity describes the Christian's unselfish willingness to give in order to make a positive difference for the purposes of Christ. Extravagant Generosity describes practices of sharing and giving that exceed all expectations and extend to unexpected measures. It describes lavish sharing, sacrifice, and giving in service to God and neighbor.

Vibrant, fruitful, growing congregations thrive because of the extraordinary sharing, willing sacrifice, and joyous giving of their members out of love for God and neighbor. Such churches teach and practice giving that focuses on the abundance of God's grace and that emphasizes the Christian's need to give rather than the church's need for money. In the spirit and manner of Christ, congregations that practice Extravagant Generosity explicitly talk about the place of money in the Christian's walk of faith. They view giving as a gift from God and are driven to be generous by a sense of mission and a desire to please God by making a positive difference in the world.

The notion that stewardship rightly focuses on the Christian's need to give rather than the church's need to receive is not simply a money-raising strategy but a spiritually powerful truth. The practice of tithing blesses and benefits the giver as much as it strengthens the mission and ministry of the church.

Americans live in an extraordinarily materialist and consumerist society. We are immersed in a culture that feeds acquisitiveness, the appetite for more and bigger, and that fosters the myth that self-worth is found in material wealth and that happiness is found in possessing. Thirty-year-olds feel like failures because they don't already have the kind of house and car that their parents own, and forty-year-olds feel unsuccessful because they're not millionaires. Millions of couples struggle under oppressive levels of debt that strain marriages, destroy happiness, and intensify conflict and anxiety. As one radio show host says, "We buy things we don't even need with money we don't even have to impress people we don't even know" (*The Dave Ramsey Show*).

2 Corinthians 8:2-4:

"They . . . gave according to their means, and even beyond their means, begging us earnestly for the privilege of sharing in this ministry to the saints."

What Is Extravagant Generosity?

Extravagant Generosity

Forty percent of the American people spend 110 percent of their annual income each year. People sustain their lifestyles through ever-increasing auto loans, credit card debt, and mortgages. When people with different incomes are asked, "How much more income would it take for you to be happy?" they answer, saying that 20 percent more income would ease their burdens, help them buy all they needed, and bring security.

Why do we feel discontent with what we have? **Happiness based on possession causes people to pursue a receding goal, leaving them dissatisfied, wanting more, and never able to satiate their desires.** At root, these are spiritual problems, not merely financial planning issues. They reveal value systems that are spiritually corrosive and that lead to continuing discontent, discouragement, and unhappiness. We can never earn enough to be happy when we believe that satisfaction, self-definition, and meaning derive principally from possessions and we can never trust our sense of self-worth when it rests on treasures that are material and temporal.

"One weekend I provided a special offering envelope during worship service. I listed a number of ministries and invited people to designate their offering to a ministry that touched their heart. Later that week, someone asked if he could talk to me about his giving. We went through the list of ministries, and because of the his genuine interest, I went on with a further list. (I think it wise to always have a long list of possibilities for people to give toward.)

The next week this person gave a check for $300,000! His family funded next year's VBS, gave toward the construction of a youth center, funded a new bus, funded upgrades for the sanctuary sound system and LCD, and contributed toward our debt.

The experience confirmed that giving people options on how

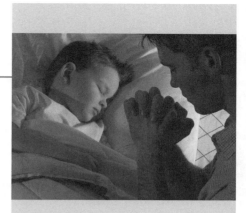

What Is Extravagant Generosity?

to give will greatly enhance funds. There are people who are very generous and simply waiting for us to ask."

—Dr. Steve Breon, Platte Woods UMC (Platte Woods, MO)

A philosophy based principally upon materialism, acquisition, and possessions is not sufficient to live by, or to die by. At some point, **followers of Jesus must decide whether they will listen to the wisdom of the world or to the wisdom of God.**

Proportional giving and tithing force people to look at their earning, saving, and spending through God's eyes. It reminds them that their ultimate worth is derived from the assurance that they are children of God, created by God, and infinitely loved by God. God's eternal love revealed in Christ is the source of self-worth; true happiness and meaning are found in growing in grace and in the knowledge and love of God.

Giving generously reprioritizes lives and helps people distinguish
what is lasting, eternal, and of infinite value from what is temporary, illusory, and untrustworthy. The discipline of generous giving places people on the balcony, helping them look out at the consumerist society with new perspective, better able to see its traps, deceptions, and myths. The practice of generosity is a means by which God builds people up, strengthens their spirits, and equips them to serve God's purposes.

Tithing helps the followers of Jesus understand that all things belong to God and that, during their days on earth, **followers are entrusted as stewards to use all they have and all they are in ways that glorify God:**

- **What Christians *earn* belongs to God,** and they should earn it honestly and in ways that serve purposes consistent with being followers of Christ.
- **What Christians *spend* belongs to God,** and they should use it wisely, not foolishly, on things that enhance life and do not diminish it.

Luke 12:13-21:

"And the things you have prepared, whose will they be? ...Take care! Be on your guard against all kinds of greed; for one's life does not consist in the abundance of possessions."

What Is Extravagant Generosity?

Extravagant Generosity

- **What Christians *save* belongs to God,** and they should invest in ways that strengthen society.
- **What Christians *give* belongs to God,** and they need to give generously, extravagantly, and conscientiously in ways that strengthen the body of Christ.

We struggle with tithing because our hearts and minds are more powerfully shaped by our affluence. We find it harder to give extravagantly because our society's values shape our perceptions more than our faith's values do.

Practice the tithe. Teach children to spend wisely, to save consistently, and to give generously. Let them learn it from their parents and grandparents so that they will be generous and not greedy, giving and not self-indulgent, charitable and not self-absorbed. Extravagant Generosity changes the life and spirit of the giver.

The practice of Extravagant Generosity also changes churches. Churches that nurture proportional giving and tithing among their members thrive. They accomplish great things for Christ, offer robust and confident ministry, and they prosper for the purposes of Christ and make a difference in the lives of people.

Every sanctuary and chapel in which we have worshiped, every church organ that has lifted our spirits, every pew where we have sat, every Communion rail where we have knelt, every hymnal from which we have sung, every praise band that has touched our hearts, every church classroom where we have gathered with our friends, every church kitchen that has prepared our meals, every church van that has taken us to camp, every church camp cabin where we have slept—all are the fruit of someone's Extravagant Generosity.

We have been the recipients of grace upon grace. We are the heirs, the beneficiaries of those who came before us who were touched by the generosity of Christ enough to give graciously so that we could experience the truth of Christ for ourselves. We owe the same to generations to come. We have worshiped in sanctuaries that we did not build, so

20

What Is Extravagant Generosity?

"Recently at New Covenant UMC, small groups were encouraged to find ministries in the community in which they could be involved. One of these groups chose to provide books to the reading classrooms of a nearby middle school where many of the children are under-privileged. An arrangement was struck with the local Barnes and Noble to provide a discount on the books and a rebate of 20% on any in-store purchases made throughout a particular week. The group also solicited contributions from the entire congregation.

Through this outreach, the small group collected over $2,000 in value of books. The school is still receiving books from the congregation, and the students are thrilled with their opportunity to read beautiful new books."

—Rev. Gary Bullock, New Covenant UMC (The Villages, FL)

to us falls the privilege of building sanctuaries where we shall never worship.

Generosity is a fruit of the Spirit, a worthy spiritual aspiration. Generosity is the opposite of selfishness, self-centeredness, and self-absorption. To practice Extravagant Generosity requires self-control, patience, kindness, faith, and love of God and neighbor. These build us up; equip us for life and for ministry; and foster perspectives and attitudes that are sustaining, enriching, and meaningful. **Giving changes both the giver and the church.**

One congregation's giving remained level for years even though the church had enjoyed moderate growth in attendance. Since the congregation continually initiated new ministries, the budget came under increased pressure; and church leaders decided to reevaluate their stewardship practices. For years, the congregation had held an October emphasis on church commitments, highlighting the membership pledge with members specifying the amount

"God has created us so we do small things with great love."

— *Mother Teresa*, Mother Teresa: In My Own Words *(Gramercy Books, 1996)*

What Is Extravagant Generosity?

Extravagant Generosity

they intended to give to support the church for the following year.

With consensus that old ways were not working well, the pastor and the finance committee began to look at new stewardship models to develop a culture of generosity. After much discussion, they agreed to common values.

First, they would not use guilt, fear, scarcity, or shame to coerce people to give. They wanted people to feel good about giving and about growing in generosity. Second, they would shift more responsibility for discussing giving from the pastor to lay members.

Third, they would emphasize the Christian's need to give rather than the church's need to receive and teach the scriptural practice of tithing and giving according to one's means. Fourth, they decided to make financial stewardship the single focus for October.

Throughout the weeks of preparation, church members shared about why they give, how they have grown in giving, and how this has affected their relationship to the church and to God. On Consecration Sunday, a guest layperson and skilled church leader from another congregation preached at both services about the significance of giving in the Christian life and about the mission of the church.

The congregation discovered that Consecration Sunday united and strengthened the church. Members felt affirmed and positive about their growth in giving. Pledges increased by more than 30 percent from the previous year's giving. The more significant benefits were the renewed fellowship, faith, and purpose that were inspired.

The keys to effective and spiritually strengthening campaigns are the same in all churches, large and small: an unapologetic but gracious emphasis on proportional giving and tithing, an emphasis on giving in the giver's walk of faith, an emphasis on the connection of money to a compelling and clear sense of mission, an emphasis on widespread participation in planning and leading, and a heavy reliance not just on the pastor but on lay leadership.

Planning Sheet

A Giving Community

How does your congregation show generosity to the community? List as many ways as you can that demonstrate this generosity outside the church walls.

_____   _____
_____   _____
_____   _____
_____   _____

What are your own church's best resources? (facility, finances, talent, location?)

_____   _____
_____   _____
_____   _____

How are these resources shared with others? _____
_____
_____

What do people in your community know about your congregation and how you interact with the community and world? What messages of generosity do you see?

_____
_____

What are three or four ways that you could raise awareness in the congregation about the importance and joy of giving?

_____   _____
_____   _____

Extravagant Generosity

SESSION 2

Planning Sheet

What are three ways you can think of now to increase giving and the level of gifts?

_____

_____

_____

What percentage of your congregation do you believe tithes? _____

What could be done through awareness, publicity, education, and inspiration to increase them more toward tithing?

_____   _____

_____   _____

_____   _____

What would the benefits would tithing bring for the congregation and individuals? How could you describe those for others? _____

_____

_____

What Can We Do?

Churches that practice Extravagant Generosity don't talk in general terms about stewardship; they speak confidently and faithfully about money, giving, generosity, and the difference giving makes for the purposes of Christ and in the life of the giver. **These churches emphasize the Christian's need to give more than the church's need for money.** They teach, preach, and practice proportional giving with the goal of tithing. They use God's name accurately by appealing to the highest of life-giving purposes for giving rather than employing fear, guilt, pressure, and shame as motivation.

They speak of joy, devotion, honoring God, and the steady growth of spirit that leads to greater generosity. They don't apologize or feel awkward as they encourage people to offer their best to God. People delight in giving. Pledge campaigns are not about money, dollars, and budgets but about mission, spiritual growth, and relationship to God.

Stewardship efforts deepen prayer life, build community, unite people with purpose, and clarify mission. People feel strengthened and grateful to serve God through giving. Extravagantly Generous congregations emphasize mission, purpose, and life-changing results rather than shortages, budgets, and institutional loyalty. They provide a compelling vision that invites people to give joyously, thereby finding purpose, meaning, and satisfaction in changing lives. They know that **God moves people to give in order to find purpose and to accomplish things for Christ.** They connect money with mission.

These churches hold high-quality annual pledge opportunities with wide participation, excellent preparation, and numerous opportunities for lay involvement. While pastors provide leadership through preaching, teaching, and example, congregations rely heavily on the witness of extravagantly generous lay persons through testimonies, sermons, newsletter meditations, and website devotionals.

Vibrant, fruitful, growing congregations focus on stewardship during the season of annual pledging; but they also emphasize faithful giving throughout the

1 Timothy 6:18-19:

"They are to do good, to be rich in good works, generous, and ready to share, thus storing up for themselves the treasure of a good foundation for the future, so that they may take hold of the life that really is life."

What Can We Do?

Extravagant Generosity

year in preaching, Bible studies, and Sunday school classes. They speak in spiritual terms about the place of wealth, affluence, acquisition, materialism, selfishness, generosity, and giving. They regularly offer members the opportunity to support causes that make a difference in lives of people, knowing that giving stimulates giving. They've learned that when special giving is aligned with the purposes of Christ, it does not diminish support for the general budget.

Pastors who nurture the practice of Extravagant Generosity express appreciation to people who give. They thank members collectively and personally, and give God thanks for increases in giving. They send personal notes of appreciation for special gifts and for unexpected increases in giving or pledging. Through quarterly reports of giving, churches that cultivate generosity keep members informed in positive and consistent ways about their pledges and their giving. Pastors, staff, and volunteers strive to cultivate trust, appreciation, and confidence with contributors.

Extravagantly Generous churches do more than encourage, teach, and support personal generosity:

• *They practice extraordinary generosity as a congregation, demonstrating exemplary support for denominational connectional ministries, special projects, and missions in their community and throughout the world.*

• *They take the lead in responding to disasters and unexpected emergencies. Lay and pastoral leadership view "giving beyond the walls" as indispensable to Christian discipleship and to congregational mission and vitality.*

• *They look for more and better opportunities to make a positive difference in the lives of people through congregational support and outreach.*

• *They make the mission of the church real, tangible, and meaningful.*

• *Their reputation for generosity extends beyond the congregation into the community.*

What Can We Do?

"Each week at Kirkwood UMC, the pastor asks everyone during the offering to give a second mile gift of ONE dollar. And each week, an example is given regarding the difference ONE can make—ONE person who touched your life, ONE ministry that touched someone's need, reminding people of the importance of giving even something small. A single mom in the church, who was struggling to raise her children on a low income, said the 'Power of ONE' ministry made her feel welcome in the church because she knew even her ONE dollar could make a difference.

When the offering plate is passed, everyone is challenged to contribute and symbolize their greater giving no matter what their giving pattern. As a result, Kirkwood UMC has realized $15,000 annually. There, something as small as ONE dollar has united the congregation, empowering them to do much more together."

—Rev. David Bennett, Kirkwood UMC (Saint Louis, MO)

Churches that grow in giving know that generosity increases with participation in ministry and community, and so they work to deepen the core ministries of worship, small-group learning, and mission. They know that many churches do not have enough money because they don't provide sufficient ministry and mission. Rather than becoming obsessed with income, survival, and maintenance, they continually return their focus to changing lives, reaching out to new people, and offering significant mission. **By growing in ministry, giving increases.**

Congregations that practice Extravagant Generosity address the challenge of growing in giving to both long-term members and those who are new to the faith. They also teach, model, and cultivate generosity among children and youth. Sunday school classes, after-school children's ministries, vacation Bible school, and youth ministries all offer opportunities to give individually and to work together in groups to achieve a ministry goal that is significant, tangible, and compelling. Rather than collecting offerings in a perfunctory way,

"O God, I will meet all kinds of people today; help me to help them all."

—*William Barclay,* More Prayers for Plain People *(Abingdon, 1962)*

What Can We Do?

Extravagant Generosity

children's and youth leaders explain, teach, and connect the action of giving to the work of God. **In churches that practice Extravagant Generosity, children and youth are taught about responsible earning, spending, saving, and giving.**

Congregations equip parents with ideas, suggestions, and practices that foster generosity for children and youth of all ages. **Congregations that cultivate generosity invite young adults into leadership and planning.** They consider contrasting patterns of earning, spending, and giving between the generations. They accommodate the church's receiving methods for gifts and pledges to the "cashless and checkless" lifestyles of members who depend upon debit cards, online banking, and wire transfers.

The pastoral and lay leadership of churches that practice Extravagant Generosity constantly learn, adapt, and improve their method of communication and teaching about giving. They attend workshops, read the literature, use consultants, study Scripture, learn about social trends and patterns of giving, and collaborate with other churches. These actions help them learn new techniques, deepen their theological understanding of giving, and foster the charitable impulse.

These churches realize that future ministry rests upon the generosity of present members and take seriously the stewardship of the resources entrusted to them by their members. Pastors and designated laity know the financial details, giving patterns, and church budget and are able to communicate accurately about the financial health of the church.

In churches that practice Extravagant Generosity, the pastor and lay leaders tithe. Proportional giving with the goal of tithing, regardless of income, becomes an expectation for those who serve in leadership roles of the church. The spiritual maturity that comes from growth in giving and the extraordinary engagement that results from tithing bring clarity of purpose and greater integrity to all the church's ministries.

The practice of Extravagant Generosity is the fruit of maturation in Christ, the result of God's sanctifying grace that molds our hearts and changes our values and behaviors.

Planning Sheet

Creating a Culture of Giving

Dave Ramsey says, "We buy things we don't even need with money we don't even have to impress people we don't even know."

In your community and congregation, what signs do you see that people are caught in a cycle of spending and debt? _____

_____

_____

What can the church do to counter the culture of consumption and over-spending? How can your congregation's ministry help people inside and outside the church value and manage their financial resources? _____

_____

_____

Taking a Next Step

List all the ways your congregation cultivates giving:

_____   _____

_____   _____

_____   _____

_____   _____

What are a few easy, simple ways to promote awareness and excitement about giving?

_____   _____

_____   _____

_____   _____

Planning Sheet

What about specifically for children?

_____   _____
_____   _____

For teens?

_____   _____
_____   _____

For visitors and community members?

_____   _____
_____   _____

Think bigger. What are one or two wide-reaching dreams that you can imagine tackling if people in your church worked together? _____
_____
_____
_____

This week, walk through the steps necessary to make one of these dreams a reality. Step by step how could your congregation undertake a dream like this?

_____
_____
_____
_____
_____
_____

Seedlings: Ideas for Ministry

"Listen! A sower went out to sow...." (Mark 4:3)

Simple, Easy, Safe Ideas • Teach, preach, and practice the tithe and proportional giving. Hold conversations about Extravagant Generosity in every adult class • Every year without exception offer a high-quality, multi-week, lay- and clergy-led, theologically sound opportunity for people to pledge and to step up their giving to support the church • Give children a chance to give • Create a giving or mission component to every VBS, children's camp, teen retreat • Ask members to share testimonies about giving and tithing • Tell stories about real people we can help through giving • Find ways to give and talk about giving with joy • Teach John Wesley's perspectives on money. Simplify your own life—spend less, want less • Tell stories from the Bible of God's extravagance • Support another congregation's food pantry (as well as your own) • Sponsor a church or pastor in another country • Send a thank-you letter from the pastor, personally signed, to each person who pledges • Teach new members how the church collects and uses money to help others • Develop a class for teens and young adults on money—earning, saving, spending, and giving, including the tithe • Write newsletter or Web articles about how the church' generosity is helping others • Ask children who have been a part of a penny project to share their results • Pray for generosity—yours and others • Celebrate milestones when funding is raised and goals are met • Include testimony and real-life responses to giving • Start a "Reading with the Pastor" book study focusing on simplicity, abundance, and giving • Support the pastor's and financial team's attendance at workshops or seminars on fundraising, generosity, and stewardship **Riskier, More Challenging Ideas** • Provide a profile of giving patterns in your congregation to help them learn how to step up toward the tithe • Create high trust, transparent, accurate, and audited financial and report systems for your congregation • Invite the finance team to read three books together about congregational giving (check out resources by Herb Miller, Michael Reeves, Willow Creek, Church of the Resurrection) • Call, talk with, email, or visit with pastors/laity from other

31

Seedlings: Ideas for Ministry

Extravagant Generosity

churches who do well cultivating congregational giving—learn from them • Read or watch videos online from well-known financial advisors—compare how they are able to communicate and educate • Send a team to visit another church that excels in giving and tithing; meet with the pastor and lay team from that church; and ask, learn, take notes, steal ideas • Host a debt-management, financial planning class to help families suffering the stress of debt • Offer helpful short-term classes on practical subjects, such as retirement planning, wills, and estate planning • Create slide shows, Web presentations and bulletin boards about the giving successes in the church • Join with another congregation in your community, state, or denomination and be a part of a major giving initiative **Big, Bold, Audacious, Scary Ideas** • Stretch toward an audacious giving goal for a project that makes a differences in people's lives and that people of all ages can support, such as Nothing but Nets, a disaster relief fund, Global Aids Fund, Africa University, a covenant church overseas. Make this the largest gift, most extravagant gift ever given by your congregation for purposes beyond your own walls. Exceed all expectations. Celebrate, share stories, party! (to the glory of God!) • Start a car ministry, refurbishing and donating cars to those who need them • Invite an evaluation and recommendations on all systems for stewardship, tithing, and generosity from an outside consultant or a pastor with expertise • Recruit a team to focus on estate planning and endowments from inside and outside the congregation, for the church, and for specific ministries • Tithe the construction costs of your new building to build a new church or clinic overseas.